Also by Edward Alderette

An Alzheimer's Journey: Carolyn's Return to Birth

Other Volumes in the Wakefulness Series:

Qualities of Searchers

Sutras: Intentions to One's Higher Power

Meditations, Contemplations and Reflections About Awareness

Volume 1 of the Wakefulness Series

Edward Alderette

ISBN-13: 978-0-9997989-1-1

1. Spiritual life-Meditations. 2. Self-help Techniques. 3. Awareness 4. Contemplation. 5. Reflection. 6. Mind and Body. I. Title

DEDICATION

I dedicate these chapters to searchers everywhere and to former teachers who contributed to this, my search.

ACKNOWLEDGMENTS

I thank my friend Cathy Carignan, my niece Eileen Knott, and my friend Mireya Hinojosa RN, for their help with the transcription, formatting and publication of my writing. Additionally, I acknowledge that Eileen Knott has gone further in the role of an agent in order to facilitate all interaction with the publishers for this book to come to be. My sincere thanks.

CONTENTS

INTRODUCTION

These chapters are about getting down some thoughts and feelings which flowed and welled up into consciousness from either meditations, or contemplations or reflections.

After I got them down I found — and keep on finding — that they have the power to propel a meditative state or a contemplative one or a significantly reflective state of being.

My hope is that each time you read, meditate, contemplate or reflect on these works that you may feel something beyond the meaning of my compositions and in the center of your experience.

What I stipulate in each of these chapters derives from personal experiences of heightened awareness. For these experiences to have occurred I needed to have placed myself in a state of conscious awareness.

Awareness can occur in one instant or it may take a struggling time for distractions to subside. What theory and direct experience have taught me is that to be aware, means to be awake to the moment. Awake to whatever is presenting itself to my attention in the given moment. Thus I can be awake to what I am observing in existence right there in front of me or what I perceive going on inside of me.

One frequently used method for becoming aware, but by no means the only one, is to focus mental attention on the breathing, i.e., the natural process going on 24/7 wherein air goes into the human body and is expelled from the human body. This constitutes focusing the mind on one motion occurring inside of oneself at that precise instant that it is occurring. It entails one actually feeling the air going in during inhalation and actually attending consciously to the air coming out in exhalation. It does not mean giving intellectual ascent to the fact that one is breathing. It means experiencing the transition of air into the chest, through the nostrils and/or mouth, through the lungs into the diaphragm where it is actually happening and to experience the exhalation motion.

The longer one can sustain mental attention on this breathing motion the more profound becomes the experience of awareness, and the less thinking of thoughts goes on. The emphasis here is that one does not concentrate on stopping thoughts; one concentrates the mind on experiencing.

There is no substitute for the repeated experience of this process. Repeated experience teaches one many things; for one, as one remains in the awakened state, there occurs a release of bodily tension (giving slack to muscles, joints, tendons) and experiencing a calm (opposite of agitated), comfortably cool (opposite of angry, irritated, irascible), collected (opposite of scattered) state of mind.

The more one goes into awareness, the more integrated it becomes for the practitioner that what one experiences is an altered state of consciousness (not unlike a daydream state).

In the altered state of consciousness, one discovers a "way of knowing" which transcends the knowing by discursive reasoning; this constitutes arriving upon a conclusion without going through the steps of induction or deduction, as in achieving an insight from an image. The distinction being made here is that knowing intuitively is different from knowing by the discursive method. Thus, awareness promotes intuition.

It is my intention to present these experiences so that the reader, by contemplating these themes, may be able to go into the awareness of the realities suggested by these themes.

The commentary at the end of each chapter is intended as a guide to further understand the recorded experiences.

CHAPTER ONE

In the vastness
Of your awareness
Allow your inner witness
To experience the permanence of impermanence
In the bitter and the sweet
In the yin and the yang
In the light and the shadow
In the here and the now
In the becoming of Being
In the vastness of
Your own awareness.

Commentary on Chapter One

This theme is not only on change but on how change is so pervasive that, in reality, no thing is simply "being." Every solitary thing, idea, event and person is changing into something else. Yet it will retain "being" (while it is always "becoming").

The suggestion here is to not only go to awareness but to follow the inner witness to the immensity which that entails so as to truly experience the pervasive change in being.

The realities of yin-yang, bitter/sweet, light/shadow, here/there, now/then etc., are daily attestations to the co-existence of opposites ever-becoming, reminding us that unless we learn to adapt (to newness) we are not relevant to life as it presents itself to us for it is forever presenting perennial change.

CHAPTER TWO

The permanence of impermanence
Is imprinted in the psyche of our Being
And comes into relief in the awareness
That this future instant
Morphing into this present instant
Which in the same flow,
Without missing a beat,
Just became the past instant,
Leaving our psyche and Being
With the intuited experience
That neither future nor present nor past exist
But only the flow (exists)
Wherein all three
Simply are and exist as one flow
Which is permanently impermanent,

In the same intuited experience
Is the awareness that our Being
Is in that flow
Which simply is.

We are in the flow,
The flow is in us.

The flow is of all there is,
Future, present and past.

Commentary on Chapter Two

The first 17 lines of this theme convey that when one reflects with a degree of awareness on any one instant in time (which we are experiencing) that act intuits for us that, in truth, the present instant is morphing into the future instant in the same instantaneity that the present just became the past instant. (Some sage pointed out that nothing is further away than one instant ago! Chapter Six also articulates this theme.)

An additional nuance here posits that since it takes but one reflective instant of awareness to intuit the one motion of "here to future to past," this intuition must be imprinted on our psyche.

That motion is here called the flow, and flow by definition is a permanent something constantly changing. Thus, the paradox in "permanence of impermanence" is experienced concretely in the flow of this instant. Intuition, to reiterate what was elaborated upon in the introduction (sixth paragraph and second to last paragraph), means knowledge acquired through experience versus knowledge acquired through thinking discursively.

A further intuited experience flowing from the above is that, indeed, the practitioner experiencing the theme of the flow realizes that he/she is likewise in the perennial flow.

The flow here is intended what is understood as the Tao in *The Tao Te Ching*, i.e. the book of the flow of integrity.

CHAPTER THREE

I want and am wanting
To go to serenity serenely,
To go to the awakening of that: Conception
                                        : Gestation
And birth of awakened awareness;
To the space between Being and becoming;
To the source of all beginnings;

To the one instant who is;

To the center of my being;
To the unfurling of my becoming;

I want and am wanting
To go to this multi-faceted experience
With: Enthusiasm
     : Inspiration and
     : Passion
Precisely so that my: Attention and
                          : Intention
For the fullness of fulfillment of Being
Grow in: Enthusiasm
       : Inspiration and
       : Passion

I want to be in the awareness
Of Being in the one instant
Who is.

Commentary on Chapter Three

This meditation considers the wanting of, now and on an ongoing basis, a multi-faceted experience. The facets desired include:

1. The state of serenity
2. The kind of awareness which comes into being the way babies do i.e. conceived, gestated and given birth to.
3. That state in where one is between "what is" and "what it just became" (as if that state were an actual space)
4. The mouth from which all flows
5. The blossoming of whatever blossoms (which includes all existence)
6. Reaching the core of the existent practitioner (that core in Hinduism is identified as "the Ultimate Reality, the root and ground of the universe, the source of "all that is").

The additional desire is for enthusiasm, passion and inspiration to accompany the original/desire (all six of the above) in order that one may grow fully in the development of one's being.

The last stanza is about the final desire. That stanza alludes to the mystery that, just as the core of my being is the Ultimate Reality so, too, that Ultimate Reality is at the core of each instant. Awareness of the instant calls forth awakening to the awareness that where the instant is so, too, is the core who is the Ultimate Reality. The final desire is to be aware of the Ultimate Reality every time the instant is intuited. Ambitious? Yes, spiritually ambitious.

CHAPTER FOUR

When you are in the vastness
Of the consciousness
Of the experience
Of awareness
You may simultaneously
Experience that that vastness
Is of Being itself.

That vastness appears to your
Enlightened consciousness
And what appears to be illuminating
You
In that instant
Is Being itself
Or a glimpse
Of the perception
Of the magnitude
Which Being is.

Commentary on Chapter Four

The bottom line of this theme is that perception (not conception), just perception of existence, is so profound and all-encompassing (vast) that our limited mind can only grasp a glimpse of that perception and we may be able to do this if our mind can go to the conscious awareness that anything is connected to everything and everything is connected to anything. Going to this connectedness is suggested as going to vastness.

What takes us to that glimpse of vastness is the experience of being consciously aware (not just conscious, but consciously aware). Many are conscious, but few are aware!!

CHAPTER FIVE

I can feel awareness
Coursing through my Being.

I can feel Being
Coursing through my awareness

Both   Happening   Occurring   Flowing   simultaneously.

I have some power
In having awareness
Coursing through my Being,

But, I know
I have no power
In the happening wherein
Being is coursing
Through my awareness.

Whatever accounts for this second flow
Is power
Separate and distinct
From me.

I rest in the belief
That it must be Being
Which accounts
For existing in me, because
I am in Being.

Commentary on Chapter Five

This experience records two separate and distinct ultra-feelings which are alluded to as "coursings." These are not physical sensations of the body. They are spoken of as having happened and flowed. They can occur simultaneously and can reoccur.

For an experience similar to this, one sets the stage by focusing centered mental attention on the awareness of sensing the presence of one's existence. That existence is the being through whom one's awareness is streaming as if the streaming were a current.

A distinction is made between that current and what happens when one is experiencing the ultra-feeling of one's existence streaming like a current through the state of one's awareness. In this case, it is noted, the one experiencing simply does so by intuiting that one is in existence while one does nothing for that presence to be. One intuits one's existence by experiencing it directly without the process of thinking. That is intuition pure and simple and not dependent on IQ.

A subtlety flowing from this is that the very awareness which one is engaging in is felt to be partaking of the streaming which is going through the state of one's awareness. The whole of Chapter 29 is an elongation of this theme of the two coursings.

The conclusion to this theme is that one can set the stage for awareness to be but not for existence. What sets the stage for my existence is that I am in existence as a fish is in water (see Chapter 8). What sets the stage for my existence is the ocean of existence in which I swim.

CHAPTER SIX

In the very same
Instant
That the
Future
Becomes the present
The present
Becomes the past
In the very same
Instant.
Thus it is that three exist in one;
Thus the eternal.

Commentary on Chapter Six

This is another way of expressing the theme presented in Chapter Two. The added nuance in this chapter is that due to the dynamic flow — present, future and past existing simultaneously — the reality presented appears as "eternity is already here."

Time is then understood to be a mental construct; it is not a reality per se but the measurement of motion.

CHAPTER SEVEN

The effulgent luminosity
Of illumination
From enlightenment
Parallels
The luminous effulgence
Of enlightenment
From illumination.

Commentary on Chapter Seven

Enlightenment and illumination are presented as two names for the same reality: one which is effulgent and luminous.

The play on words intends to highlight the presence of light in the reality of awakening: the light of being awake.

CHAPTER EIGHT

There once was a fish
In an ocean
Who had this unusual
Notion,
That the sea he was in
Was a sea within him
And would not dispel
That emotion.

Aside: Consciousness is not in us
Anymore than the ocean
Is in the fish; we are in
The ocean of consciousness.

The paradigm is buddhistic
The limerick is mine.

Commentary on Chapter Eight

(The commentary is in the aside to the limerick). In short, the consciousness we are "in" is not of our own making. (See commentary to Chapter Five).

Mystic thought takes this theme further positing that we are in fact consciousness — pure consciousness.

CHAPTER NINE

In order to have
An appreciation
Of the: Depth and
*   : Beauty and*
*   : Vastness and*
*   : Meaning*
*   Of life,*

You go
To the: Depth and
*   : Beauty and*
*   : Vastness and*
*   : Meaning*
*   Of Being.*

You go to the Being
Whom you are,
The Being you go to
Is your Being.

You derive
The meaning
Of Being
By putting yourself
In the presence
Of Being.

In that presence
You feel the
Depth and Beauty
And Vastness and
Meaning of life.

And if you were to inquire
"How often must I go to the presence
Of the presence?"
Being itself responds:
As frequently as
You want this appreciation!

Commentary on Chapter Nine

The root question of all of humankind's philosophies is a variant of the question: "What is life?" This chapter suggests that to know where to begin to explore the depth, beauty, vastness and meaning of life, one need go no further than to the existence (being) which one experiences as oneself: "you go to your being, I go to mine."

This suggests that there is no meaning to life outside of life itself, so, we go to the life we are experiencing.

In the awareness of this experience (of one's life while it is going on), one comes upon the reality that the mystery we are pondering (like all mystery) is infinitely knowable, i.e., when we ponder life, we are pondering the infinite. The Center for Action and Contemplation's Richard Rohr posits this theme in many of his daily meditations. Appreciation for the source of life's depth, beauty, vastness and meaning comes from this pondering of the infinite.

CHAPTER TEN

I am the one instant who is
And my experience reveals it to me,
In one flash of an awareness
While I am in a state of meditation.
In this intuited experience
I am aware of the power of feeling
(And not the power of knowing)
That the me I experience
In awareness
Is an instant
And the instant I feel
Is the me of my Being and
The Being of my me.

Thus the instant who is
Has neither past nor future
As if once in existence
It co-exists with
The eternity of Being
And the Being of eternity.

In the awareness of instantaneity
And the instantaneity of awareness
One is out of space-time continuum
Thus in the eternal instant.

Commentary on Chapter Ten

Had the experiences recorded here taken place in the order which we have in ordinary consciousness instead of as they do occur in an altered state of consciousness, this chapter would read as follows!

In the awareness of instantaneity and the instantaneity of awareness, one is "out of the space/time continuum," and, thus, in the eternal instant (no time, therefore eternity).

Instantaneity co-exists with eternity. To be aware of instantaneity is to be awake to the daily experienceable fact that each present instant is becoming the future one and does so as it simultaneously becomes the past instant. What results from this ongoing dynamic is that there is no time, only the eternal instant (see commentary to Chapter Six).

In the intuited experience of this "out of space/time continuum," one's experience is that the self and the instant are one, just like experiencing self and awareness are one. And because the instant and the self are experienced as one (in that altered state of consciousness and beyond ordinary awareness), I, as the author of the experience recorded, can address the feeling (not the sensation) that the instant which I am feeling is the instant of my being and the being of me.

Every time this mystery (the mystery of eternity) is addressed in this writing, the intent is to explore further this reality which is "infinitely knowable."

The discussion here also rests on the scientific definition of time being: "the measurement of motion" and opposite of eternity. The motion our scientific community measures is none other than the movement of our earth in its orbit around our solar system. (A surprising number of adults do not avert to this scientific fact).

The intent here is not to squeeze all of eternity into one instant, but to expand the instant to encapsulate the admittedly "unencapsulable." (It is the human mind dealing with a mystery).

CHAPTER ELEVEN

D'ja ever wonder who made you?
One plausible answer is that powers
Of the universe conspired in the
Making of you.

Why did powers of the universe
Conspire to make you?
One plausible answer is, they
Conspired to make you
To feel.

You feel through the life you have.
That life is energy.
The energy allows you to feel.
You can feel the energy of life
By being alive.

That energy is power of and from
The universe.
You partake of that power.
You were made to partake,
You fulfill a purpose in life
By being alive.
Feeling life is being alive.

It is through awareness that
The feeling occurs.

Awareness is feeling life.

Commentary on Chapter Eleven

The first line of the first stanza asks one of the most fundamental questions of all philosophical systems, namely: "Where do I come from?" Here the question is posed in the form: "Who made me?"

The universe, through its powers, is quickly identified as my plausible author of life, and this, simply because I am made of universal elements.

The next stanza asks a follow-up question to, "Where do I come from?" "Why was I made; why was I created and endowed with existence, given the essence who I feel I am?"

Then, quickly, a plausible explanation is that, perhaps, I was made to feel - to feel existence! To feel me in existence!

The reason it is plausible that one was made to feel is simply because we do feel and we "do this feeling" through the life we are living and do so because we are energy in existence. This existing energy comes from the nourishment of the universe and in this way, we are partaking of universal existence which can then be taken as a purpose fulfilled. The purpose being: to partake of the universe.

To be awake to all of this is to be consciously experiencing life.

None of what is said here is intended to make it easy to define what awareness is. It is suggested that awareness is feeling life, i.e., living reflectively.

In these ages of science it is easier to accept the plausibility of the powers of the universe as the agents responsible for our existence. Society, by and large, still attributes cause and effect powers to unseen presumed gods and goddesses.

Because of science in our age, it may be less easy to grasp why we were brought out of non-existence to be in existence.

Here it is postulated that "plausibly we were made to feel." To feel life. To feel that which we were given: namely, existence.

Feeling, energy and power are then all grouped, tied together and all traced to the universe. Partaking of one, we are partaker of all three.

More importantly, being alive means being all three. Not "having" feeling, energy and power, but "being" feeling, energy and power.

Feeling life occurs through awareness and from that it flows that awareness is feeling life. Buddhism states simply that awareness is being awake. This meditation elaborates on what one is awake to: namely, feeling life.

CHAPTER TWELVE

As a traveler in life in one section
Of the universe, you are receiving, totally
Free, the gift of time and energy.

These are the two absolute values
Of your life (as was observed by
Buckminster Fuller): all else is
Of relative value.

Neither you nor I could have done
Anything to deserve this time and
Energy which constitutes our life.

It was given to us freely for reasons
Totally apart and outside of our
Experience.

Once in the vastness of life's purview
We have the freedom to use
Our time and energy to pursue
Health
Wealth and
Happiness and we have the right
To exercise that freedom.

It is ours also to seek and to hold onto:
Love,
Respect and

Appreciation.

Never ever in our one lifetime
Will neither you nor I be able
To have the whole pie of life,
Meaning the pie of:
Healthwealthhappinessloverespectand/orappreciation

But you and I are entitled
To our fair share of the economy of the pie of
Life,
As long as we're not interfering
With the right of our fellow-traveler
To pursue his/her fair share of
The pie of life.

Commentary on Chapter Twelve

This chapter posits seven deep concepts for our reflection.

1. Whenever we are in this life (as if it were a journey), we are receiving time and energy. (Time, in this context, is the measurement of motion. Energy is the ultimate stuff of life).

2. The visionary Buckminster Fuller is credited with the observation that these two ingredients of human life constitute the only two absolute values and that all else is of relative value only.

3. These absolute values are not earned by us humans but freely bestowed.

4. A gift which accompanies the bestowal of these two values is that we have the freedom to choose how to use those two values. The implication is there that we have no choice but to accept this gift! We are condemned to choose, as the existentialists proclaim.

5. We can choose time and energy to pursue any or all of a) health b) wealth c) happiness d) love e) respect f) appreciation. These are not exclusionary of other pursuits; they are representative of what we can use time and energy to pursue.

6. We will not have 100% of these pursuits; nevertheless, we are entitled to our fair share.

7. The fair share is indicated by one pursuing as much as one cares to, provided one does not step on someone else's well-founded title (right) to their fair share.

CHAPTER THIRTEEN

Engage your mental attention
With one of the natural rhythms
Of your own body
Aligning that focus
On how it is feeling
Right now
To expand and contract
As your chest goes up
And your chest goes down
As air goes in
And some air comes out
And you convert oxygen from air
Into breath of life.

Commentary on Chapter Thirteen

This chapter calls attention to the singularly most important motion (certainly, the most immediate) going on in the entire universe relative to our being alive. That is the motion of normal breathing which, of course constitutes air going in and out of one's body and causing rhythmic expansion and contraction of the lungs and chest.

It is the intelligence of the lungs and the respiratory system which makes the breathing motion the most important motion in the whole universe relative to our B-E-I-N-G A-L-I-VE. Because in that motion the body takes in oxygen in the breathed-in-air and distributes it to every cell in the human body. Without that oxygen, those cells die. The living body depends on living cells.

The motion is simple to experience; one need only focus mental attention on the lungs. What is effortlessly experienced is that ordinary air is transformed into breath of life. The word "transformation" is used because air is of the material world and breath is of the spirit world — the incorporeal, the non-local, the spiritual

Our body accomplishes this transformation 24 hours a day and seven days a week, from birth to the day of death or lack of breathing.

CHAPTER FOURTEEN

On the day you were born
Life gave to you
A mountain to climb
And
A road to get there
To it.

What comes with that mountain
And
The road that leads right
To it
Is that
You know neither the day
On which you will die, and die you will
Nor is it obvious
Why you were given life
— A meaning to be sought by you —
Nor do you know
How you will choose to live,
But choose you must
And you will not know
The absolute way
To not be lonely
But only relative ways
Will be your lot.

Commentary on Chapter Fourteen

The metaphor in this chapter is that life is like a road (Tao) and that this road is to lead us to a certain mountain to climb.

Four certainties, in the form of four existential givens, are presented as accompanying our road and mountain to be climbed:

1. We may neither know when nor where, but it is certain that our life will end. Our road is not for forever.

2. Nor is it obvious what the purpose is for the life we were given.

3. No one can give us our purpose in life. Ultimately, we choose — freely or under duress — but we choose.

4. We will find only relative ways to put a boundary on pain and suffering; no absolute way is ever found by anyone. We will always have this limitation to contend with. As with loneliness, we find only relative ways of taming it, never an absolute one.

CHAPTER FIFTEEN

Inner space
Is
As infinite
As
Outer space
Just the opposite
Direction.

Commentary on Chapter Fifteen

This chapter simply observes that one can peer into infinity with the eyes wide open and, looking as far as the eyes can see, knowing we'll never see a boundary. Then, one can close the eyes of the body and, with the mental vision we possess, "peer" into the inner space and "see" that it, too, stretches into infinity. One is looking out; one is looking in.

This is an existential fact which can be verified by our own experience at anytime. Awareness of it can lead to an experience of awe.

CHAPTER SIXTEEN

You go to the sacred space
Inside of you
To hear the quietness
Of tranquility
To sense the stillness
Of serenity
To feel the oneness
Of peacefulness
And to be in the
Tranquility of quietness
And in the
Serenity of stillness
And in the
Peacefulness of oneness,
In the sacred space
Inside of you.

Commentary on Chapter Sixteen

The bottom line of this meditation theme is that one can experience (arrive upon the experience) the state of being at one (in oneness) with "all that is."

This narrative suggests that one way of arriving upon oneness is to place the self in sacred space, i.e., inside of one's awareness, and, once there, seek quietness (and attend to that quietness) — the quietness of what we can imagine tranquility to be.

We literally are asked to actively imagine what tranquility is. From that experience, one proceeds to just be in the tranquility of quietness. Just be in quietness. Just being in tranquility.

Next, staying in that state of awareness, search (inside one's self) for the stillness of one's body while deliberately releasing physical tension. From this arises the serene state brought on by awareness (itself) of the stillness. One's awareness can move to experience the serenity of stillness. It requires the imagination to be employed.

Truly, one can then experience peacefulness from the amalgamation of quietness and stillness and, in that peacefulness, one can feel at one with everything almost as naturally as quietness and stillness have become one inside the awake self.

CHAPTER SEVENTEEN

You can hear
The quietness in tranquility
When you descend to the floor,
The floor of that mystical canyon
Inside of you
Whose walls are
Being on one side and
Becoming on the opposing one.
And your presence in that vortex of energy
Can be
Where music was
Before someone's inspiration
Breathed it into existence
And where language
Flowed amorphously
Before human intelligence
Organized it
Into intelligible thought and
Verbalized feeling
And where the sounds of nature
- like thunder
And the roar of an ocean
Were tamed
To await their grand entrance
Into the world of the hearing.

That vortex
Is the state of tranquility.
In that vortex of energy
Between your Being and your becoming
To which only the vehicle
Of awareness
Can take you,
Is
Where you are
In the great quietness
Which antecedes music
And language
And the compressions of air
For which nature
Is responsible.
The quietness is in the
Sacred space
Inside of you.

Commentary on Chapter Seventeen

Chapter 17 composes a myth, by way of a metaphor, that there exists, inside of you (nowhere else), a canyon. This canyon is mystical in that it can propel you to an awakening of a dimension beyond the one to which our senses take us. Science calls that dimension quantum reality. It is also known as virtual reality.

The myth goes on to say that the walls of this canyon are "being" on one side and "becoming" on the other and that between them there is a vortex of energy. The myth does not say outright that the vortex is enchanted, but it implies it, stating that when one goes there — to the imagined vortex — one is where music exists in potency awaiting to be actualized.

Actualization takes place because of one's inspiration, just as actualization of language (which also flows amorphously i.e., without shape or form but as a possibility) is breathed into existence.

Chapter 17 is telling us that if we were to take all sounds, music, speech and the sounds of nature back to where they were before they existed, we would be in the quietness of tranquility i.e., a vortex between existence and non-existence.

CHAPTER EIGHTEEN

In the sacred space
Inside of you
You can sense the
Stillness of serenity
When you experience
The paradoxical
"stillness in slow motion
And slow motion in stillness"
Which occurs
In that instant
Of clock time
When you are aware
Of movement
At its slowest
And in the state of
Becoming the essence
Which serenity
Is,
In the sacred space
Inside of you.

Commentary on Chapter Eighteen

Once again, I call the space inside of you sacred. I mean to say that it is a place deserving to be reverenced because, to the awakened cognoscenti, it is a place evoking reverence.

This contemplation suggests that you try to experience paradox (just like one does ever so effortlessly in a night dream when the dreamer accepts the coexistence of contradictory elements without a question).

I introduce the Buddhistic paradox of "stillness in slow motion" and assert that, while you ponder that particular paradox, you will sense a mood arising within you — a mood which quickly becomes a state of experiencing a clock-time moment when movement itself slows down to become a moment of serenity instead of a moment going somewhere. It is a moment of having arrived at stillness. i.e., much like being in between the beginning and the end of the moment.

The stillness is also the space between slowly moving moments — ever so slowly moving moments. Of equal significance is that this experience occurs in one's sacred space. This experience is not reserved for a select few.

CHAPTER NINETEEN

In the sacred space
Inside of you
Where you go to the
Peacefulness
Of oneness
You encounter
And
Are encountered
Be the oneness of
Your mind and your body;

By the oneness of your inner witness
With your perception of what
You witness in your outer world;

By the oneness of your
Being with your becoming;

By the oneness of your consciousness
With the universal consciousness;
By the oneness of the universe
With your inner-verse;

And you encounter and are encountered
By the oneness of the spirit of your Being
With the oneness of the spirit of all Being,
In the oneness of peacefulness
In the sacred space inside
Of you.

Commentary on Chapter Nineteen

This chapter speaks to quite a profound meditative state where one can experience peacefulness as a oneness — a oneness that manifests itself in six (at least six) forms!

1. The oneness of the mind and the body,
2. The oneness of the inner witness and the witness taking in what appears external to oneself,
3. The oneness of the existent and that which it is turning into (becoming),
4. The oneness of the sea of universal consciousness and its participating individual/consciousness within it,
5. The oneness of inner and outer life and
6. The oneness of one's individual unifying principle with the unifying principle permeating all reality.

Another level to this meditation is that one comes upon these six forms and one is simultaneously "come upon" by these six forms.

More than an intellectual exercise is implied here. It is an experience where one is simultaneously the agent and the recipient of the oneness experienced. It is not implied but categorically stated that this entire experience results from, first, going to one's sacred space (centeredness) and, from that, experiencing peacefulness within the self.

Some would argue that it is in the heart and not the mind where one encounters peace; it is not in the thinking-self but in the feeing-self. I rather favor this argument.

One last reminder in the chapter is that all this occurs within a ground (space) considered sacred. That is the feeling-self.

CHAPTER TWENTY

When you have set
The conditions just right
For your focused consciousness
To move
To your inner space
You have consciously moved
To awareness
Wherein consciousness
Is experienced
With all the force and power
Of now.
Thus
Now and awareness
Are melded
In oneness.

Commentary on Chapter Twenty

This chapter comments on our consciousness and its ability to move to inner space i.e., to another level of being — one we refer to as inner space.

It concedes that we do not have to know how to go to that other level. What we need to know are the conditions to set and how to set them for consciousness itself to go there. This all happens just as when we set the conditions for going to sleep. Sleep happens when we set the conditions just right. Similarly, with awareness, we set the conditions (just right) by first focusing our consciousness on the present — the now — the immediate at hand. In so doing, our consciousness can naturally slip into an awakened state — awake to the power and force of the now.

In the presence of the now, one is melding now and "the awakening." I awaken to the oneness which now is. This suggests that we become one with now if only in a limited way. Limited though it may be, the more frequently we go there, the more our awakening deepens and heightens (paradox intended!).

CHAPTER TWENTY-ONE

The Beginning of All Sources
Who is the Source of All Beginnings
Has been demonstrating to us

Through life's   patterns   cycles   laws   that every

 Alpha is heading towards its own
Omega and that same author
Of the stuff of life
Has been revealing to us how
Cyclical-ness by nature (i.e. the
Observable flow of things) entails
The ability of each omega
To transmogrify itself into a
Brand new alpha
(thesis becoming its Hegelian Antithesis)
All of which hints that the
Beginning of All Sources and
The Source of All Beginnings
Is the original alpha and omega.

Commentary on Chapter Twenty-One

This chapter offers for contemplation that the observable patterns and cycles of nature are consistent enough to be regarded as laws of life. These patterns point to the existence of an author and that author can rightly be regarded as the beginning of all sources and the source of all beginnings which makes that author superior to the laws of nature.

In the observable cyclical-ness of nature it is evident to the observer (you and I) that, in the flow of things (since everything is in the perpetual motion of change), every ending goes into a new beginning — from the end of this instant to the beginning of another instant to the end of a season to the beginning of a predictable one until we arrive upon a pattern of seasons. The pattern remains permanent, while everything contained in the pattern is constantly becoming/changing.

This theme is addressed in Hegel's philosophy as he posits that every proposition in nature contains its opposite and that only by understanding both (opposites) can one understand what they both contribute to "what is." Thesis morphs into anti-thesis then transforms to synthesis which becomes the new thesis; so, the cyclical pattern goes on.

The final note for contemplation is simply that the author of beginnings and endings originated the dialectic and reveals it all to us by the observable (experienceable) patterns in nature right before our eyes.

CHAPTER TWENTY-TWO

When you experience awareness
You do so at a level deeper than
Where the mind can go.

This is to say,
You can go deeper than your mind
Can.

The aware-experience, i.e. awareness,
Begins and ends at the inner most
Being where your inner witness is.
That is the threshold whence
Becoming is issuing forth from
Being itself.

That threshold is at that
Deeper level of intelligence
Whom you are and the
Intelligence in whom
You participate.

In the awareness of your Being
And of the becoming of your
Being
You have a glimpse of the
Awareness of the Being
Which all that is becoming
Is.

In the awareness of your
State of Being
You are in the state of your
Becoming
In every instant
That is and
Is becoming.

And the awareness of
The state, which all this puts you in,
Your inner witness can have
A profound perception
Of those two primary tools with
Which and through which you
Manifest your existence,
Namely, the body in which your reside
And the mind which operates
In that body.

The body you experience is the
tool which you use to derive
the sentient experiences of
light and sound and smell and
taste ad all that the tactile
embraces.

And in the awareness of these 5 physical senses
You come alive to the
Simple reminder
That those are your vehicles
For contact with the outside world
And the vehicles through which
The outside comes into you by way
Of photons and compressions of air and
Molecules carrying fragrances and
Tastes which awaken buds of taste
And by way of surfaces which convey
Softness and roughness and
Wetness and dryness
Etc., etc., et cetera.

The mind you experience
Is that functioning within you
Which you find yourself employing
In the dialectics of reaching conclusions
Via induction and deduction.
In that awareness
Of your Being and your becoming
You also can perceive
With more clarity than normal
That indeed,
The intelligence who you are
Can also arrive upon conclusions
And can do so without the
Machinations of inducing and
Deducing
And is doing just that
In those moments which we call
Moments of enlightenment
Or moments of insight or
Leaps of intuitiveness or
Bursts of creativity.

Commentary on Chapter Twenty-Two

Some human experiences cannot be proved by reason alone. This may account for human kind's invention of poetry. Poetry says more by what it suggests than by what it says outright. What it suggests is not said; it is suggested.

Awareness, this chapter suggests, is one of those experiences which only one's experience of it suggests its essence. In a poetic sense it can be said that, when we are in awareness, we are so far deep in our intelligent self that it is "as if" we are where the principle of becoming is actually arising from the principle of our very being.

Reasoning, it is suggested, is a faculty of our intelligence but there is a faculty for knowing of things more profound than reason at its best. As J. Philip Newell has written, "…in the soul of every human being there are depths beyond naming and heights greater than knowing…"[1]

The fourth paragraph adds another dimension to our intelligence: the act of awareness is a participation in a higher intelligence.

The fifth paragraph simply posits that we cannot experience "being" that is external to us. We can know about it but not experience it directly. We derive a glimpse of what it takes for other beings to have awareness, and that glimpse comes from our own experience of our own being (existence).

Paragraphs six and seven speak to the awareness that our existence is a "becoming" existence. i.e., not a static but a dynamic one. Paragraph seven addresses specifically that our dynamic-self exists through the medium of a body and a mind. We are neither our body nor our mind. Those two entities are as tools through which we are in contact with our reality.

For the sake of contemplation, the body is delineated as a tool through which the outside reality enters the self via photons, compressions of air, fragrances, tastes and surface textures.

---

[1] J. Philip Newell, *Sounds of the Eternal: A Celtic Psalter*. Wm. B. Eerdmans Publishing Co, 2002: page 4.

The mind is delineated as "the functioning" way we reach conclusions about our world by the reasoning tools induction and deduction.

The final paragraph goes beyond, saying that mind and body are tools of the self. It asserts that, in meditative awareness, one is awareness itself. In awareness, we are arriving upon the understanding of realities through a moment we can call a paradigm shift, a revelation, an inspiration, an insight, an intuition or an experience of the non-local domain.

Only experience itself can prove to us that these moments exist. They all occur at a level deeper than the realm where reason dwells, i.e., they exist at a level beyond where the mind can go.

CHAPTER TWENTY-THREE

From the awareness of now
You can perceive yourself in the
Awareness of Being and in this
State you are looking into the
Face of the mystery of all that is
And what you are seeing in your
Own inner space goes on and on
Forever and in all directions
As if you were negotiating endless
Space where nothing exists
And paradoxically
Where all that is, is.

In that precise endlessness
Of nothingness and everything-ness
You are in the presence
Of Being
Before the awakening
Of becoming,
All in the mystery of
What life is.

Commentary on Chapter Twenty-Three

The experience recorded here is about a phenomenological awareness of being (versus an intellectual awareness) that one arrives upon by "going" to the awareness of the (ever present) now.

In this experiential awareness of being (existence), one is in the face of mystery pure and simple. This mystery might be described by the sage as: "a reality we can perceive but cannot conceive."

In an effort to suggest what the face of this mystery reveals, the narrative speaks to "the timeless and formless." Eckhart Tolle cautions that "[The Now] is your only point of access into the timeless and formless realm of being."[2] Reference to "...endless space where nothing exists, and paradoxically where all that is, is" is intended to suggest endlessness and formlessness in this narrative.

The last sentence suggests that if you can imagine the "endlessness of nothingness" you can imagine being without becoming (existence that isn't moving). This obvious impossibility speaks to the mystery of what life is: the mystery of existence and the mystery of every-thingness and its opposite — the mystery of all that exists.

---

[2] Eckhart Tolle, *The Power of Now: A Guide to Spiritual Enlightenment*. New World Library and Namaste Publishing Co., 1999: page 49.

CHAPTER TWENTY-FOUR

You
Feel
The power
Of Being
By Being
In the power
Of feeling
And
When you feel
The power
Of Being
You are
The Being
You feel.

Commentary on Chapter Twenty-Four

The first part of this chapter extols feeling versus knowing. It suggests: "put yourself in the mode of feeling your existence if you want to feel the power which your existence bestows upon you."

It suggests further: when you are aware of this power, you are the real you who is underneath the masks ascribed by your knowing self (versus your feeling self). The knowing self is all about the surface stuff; the feeling self is about the substratum.

Science talks about quantum physics or virtual reality as the reality which underlies the material, measurable reality. In a similar vein, this chapter speaks to the revelation of "you" beyond the material, measurable you.

CHAPTER TWENTY-FIVE

I Feel
  Feel
  Feel
  The Power
      Power
      Power
           Of Being
           Being
           Being
I AM
 AM
 AM
    The Being
      Being
      Being
         I Feel
         Feel
         Feel.

Commentary on Chapter Twenty-Five

This chapter picks up, like a drumbeat, the last line of Chapter 24: when you feel (versus know) the richness of who you truly are, you arrive upon the experience of being exactly what you feel (experience) even if words can only suggest your experience as the "who" you are underneath the masks of, say, the knowing world.

CHAPTER TWENTY-SIX

When your awareness
Flows through your Being
You will experience
That the Being
Flowing through you
Is greater than your awareness
Or
That the Being flowing
Through your awareness
Is greater than you.

Commentary on Chapter Twenty-Six

In the normal course of events, when one is in the state of awareness (which is out of the course of normal events) and when that awareness is focused on one's being (existent self), the resulting experience takes the form of the existent self being the owner of the state of awareness (two distinct entities). This would make awareness a possession of one's being, so to speak.

The second part of the meditation (after the "or") goes on to state that the existent self is more "you" than the you on whom your awareness can focus.

All together, this piece states that one cannot be fully aware of the true nature of what one really is in the normal course of events. There is more mystery to what or who one really is than meets the human intelligence.

CHAPTER TWENTY-SEVEN

One vehicle
To an experience of enlightenment
Is to be in the awareness
Of consciousness
In the awareness of Being.

From this can flow
An experience
Of what quietness is
In the vastness
Of the state one is in
In the quietness
Of sheer vastness.

Commentary on Chapter Twenty-Seven

This meditation distinguishes between consciousness and awareness, and the human agent of these two states of being. The human being can be in consciousness but not in awareness. This means one's intelligence can be thinking about mental constructs it has formulated about reality. When one uses one's consciousness in order to be awake to what reality is i.e., experiencing reality versus focusing on mental constructs about it, one is in the mental state of consciousness and awareness. To be in these two states is to experience enlightenment.

When one is attempting to be awake "to what is," one is perforce attempting to wrap the focus around omnipresence and omni-direction, and, here, this is called vastness. It can be akin to attempting to be awake to total quietness — awake to what is present where there exists a total absence of sound.

For background sake, note: a dictum in epistemology states that the human mind is capable of going to three degrees of abstraction. The first degree entails thinking about a genus; i.e., a class to which many particulars belong (e.g., chair and table belong under my abstraction furniture).

The mind is in the second degree when it is thinking mathematically (2+2=4; two plus two anythings equal four anythings); the third degree takes the mind to thinking about being and the laws of being (metaphysics).

With the phrase "...awareness of being," this meditation speaks to experiencing "being" (versus thinking about it) and the act of consciousness in so doing. The statement "...an experience of enlightenment" alludes to going to an altered state of consciousness; one way (vehicle) to getting there exists in experiencing "being" (versus thinking about it). It is not the mind going to the experience of being. It is the consciousness. This is not a new degree of abstraction simply because it is not the mind doing it; it is the consciousness doing it.

The second stanza alludes to a concomitant experience

in which felt consciousness, rather than the mind, is able to morph (as it were) between quietness and vastness and back again from vastness to quietness).

Consciousness in awareness renders experiences separate and distinct from a thinking consciousness.

I wholeheartedly concur with the observation that all language related to the experience of enlightenment is inadequate and unable to convey that with which awareness puts one in touch.

CHAPTER TWENTY-EIGHT

Awareness is to enlightenment
As common sense
Is to wisdom.
Thus:
When you have common sense
You already have at least
The beginning of wisdom,

For what else is wisdom
If not the exploration
Of the sense in the common.

In like manner
Awareness
Is like the waking up
Needed
To be in the consciousness
Of what is enlightening.

The one contains the other
And the other
Is but a dimension
Of the one.

Commentary on Chapter Twenty-Eight

This experience puts into relief the kinship between common sense and wisdom and the consideration that the one contains the second and the first is but a dimension of the second.

That kinship is next juxtaposed to the kinship between enlightenment and awareness. Again, not only is there contained in the second kinship the consideration that the one contains the other while the other is but a dimension of the one, but also subtly suggested is that the two kinships contain each other and each is but a dimension of the one.

The invisible concatenation implied is that common sense leads to wisdom while wisdom leads to the wakefulness which takes one to enlightenment.

CHAPTER TWENTY-NINE

When you are in the awareness
Of your Being
You can feel Being coursing
Through your awareness,

And simultaneously you experience
Awareness
Coursing through the Being
Whom you are.

One gateway to this awareness
Is to feel and sense and experience
Through focusing and centering,
On first, the blood moving
Through your circulatory system
Which of course courses
Throughout your body,

And it is when you find your mind
Making its way to all-of-you-parts
That you can then be aware
Of the Being who is comprised
Of all-of-those-you-parts
And who is the unifying principle
Of the circulatory motion
Which is inextricably connected
To the expansion and contraction
Movement
Of the pump we call the heart

Of the body human,
The very organ which originates
The push and pull
Of aortas and arteries and veins
And capillaries
Whose pull and push activity
Results in the coursing
Of the fluid, blood
And activates the consciousness
— your consciousness —
To the experience
Of coursing:
Being coursing through your
Awareness
Awareness coursing through
Your being
So cyclically, so effortlessly
So naturally
In the eternal moment of now —
Right now.

Commentary on Chapter Twenty-Nine

Straight up no-nonsense, unadulterated prose would render this chapter this way: blood is coursing through your entire body and all the parts of your body are affected by this circulatory motion.

The circulation goes on due to a pump we call the heart (some call it a muscle) and the expansion and contraction of a whole network of blood vessels of various sizes from aortas to capillaries. (Implied: there is something awesome here). Now, focusing the mental attention on this circulatory motion (called the coursing) awakens the one focusing to be aware of the phenomenon that is not just the flow of blood but a coursing of existence (itself) throughout the agent of the focus. "Being coursing through your awareness."

To experience that one's existence is flowing, as if it were a material current of some sort, is to be experiencing at a more profound level than when one is experiencing the flow of one's circulatory system. The flow of blood is a sensation. The flow of one's existence is an emotion of feeling — one's reaction to one's own cognition.

And, then, to be aware of a happening which entails the flow of a current of experience itself (as if "experiences" were a material which can flow as material currents do) speaks to a more profound level of wakefulness than when one is in ordinary awareness to currents of the body. This other awareness is in the spiritual world; it is awareness of a spiritual reality (one outside the material world).

And the experience proclaims that it can all be lived through (experienced) effortlessly and in accord with one's nature; i.e., there is nothing supernatural about it. It is natural to be able to experience spiritual awareness.

And these coursings are all in progress right now. They are ready to be experienced: now. (See Chapter Five for a separate rendition on these two coursings.)

CHAPTER THIRTY

In the mood
Of inspiration
Which comes from an energy
Higher than that of consciousness
I am finding myself
To be wanting to effectuate
Whatever it takes
To dispose
Whatever it takes
For beauty to emerge
From simplicity
And for simplicity
To unfurl from beauty.
Thusly:
I participate
In the creative process.

Commentary on Chapter Thirty

This narrative assumes that inspiration arises from a mood and that that mood is from an energy source which is superior to (or different from) the energy of consciousness. Another assumption is that consciousness is an energy field. (No name is immediately given to the superior/different energy).

This narrated experience proclaims that, in the mood of inspiration, the inspired one is prepared to bring about whatever is needed in order to set the conditions right for beauty to issue forth from something simple and the (simultaneous) unfurling of simplicity from beauty.

This (the above) is how one participates in creativity — a process which goes on outside of the participant (i.e., the inspired one). That process is referred to as the creative process. This is the name of the energy superior/different from consciousness.

That creative process is subtly presented as containing: 1) the inspiration to create, 2) the one being inspired and 3) the act needed (from the inspired) for the inspiration to result in beauty that emerges from simplicity and simplicity that unfurls from beauty.

CHAPTER THIRTY-ONE

Your immersion in the awareness
Of the harmony of the universe
Will generate
The peace which the universe
Exudes
Even in the chaos of
The moment;

For the vehicle which
Awareness is
Can take you
To the energy
Which is peace
In the progression
Of harmoniousness.

Commentary on Chapter Thirty-One

This is a statement on "feeling" states, not states of "knowing." To be "immersed in awareness" is to be in a state conducive of transformation, as opposed to information. And to be immersed in the awareness of harmony of the universe is to feel (not know) the harmony whence comes the vibration of universal peace, even when, in one sector of existence, chaos seems to dominate.

The transforming state (awareness) is the point at which one arrives upon peace that could only be present as a result of harmony in progress.

CHAPTER THIRTY-TWO

Long has
The spirit
Of the soul
Of your Being
Searched for a niche.
One niche in the whole wide world
One just barely big enough to comfortably
Accommodate your body and its four limbs
Without being crowded but hugged
And snuggled in total safety
And pure security.

And in that safety and security
Of that niche
You want to have time sufficient
To go inwardly and to be aware
Of only the enveloping niche
Which embraces you
In that instant where
There is no future
Where there is no past
Only the instant of embrace
Which is embracing
the instant of being embraced
And held in the warmth
Of all that converges
Upon the receptacle of space
Holding your body and its four limbs,
You

Going deeper and deeper
Into the recesses
Of the spirit
Of the soul
Of the Being
Who you are.

Commentary on Chapter Thirty-Two

In the first sentence, this chapter calls for an imaginary space which can serve as a cocoon that tightly, comfortably and safely secures one contemplative searcher.

In the second sentence we see how the searcher materializes what was — a moment ago — an imaginary space. Once in the materialized cocoon, the searcher has gone inward to contemplate the moment (no future, no past) in which they are literally enveloped. The searcher stays in the instant (stays in the moment) feeling (experiencing) all that converges in the embrace of the body while the experiencing self finds a path to the recesses of who the searcher is — their being. (Spoiler: it is the now (the instant, that is) that converges in the embrace of the searcher's body and the experiencing self).

CHAPTER THIRTY-THREE

You
Are
The Being
You feel
When
You
Are feeling
The Being
You
Are.

Commentary on Chapter Thirty-Three

Reminiscent of Chapters 23, 24, and 33, this chapter strikes the chord that, if the being who you are is, say, pure consciousness, you will be experiencing that pure consciousness when you put yourself in the awareness of the pure consciousness.

Cognoscenti in matters of the spirit remind us that awareness is a state of transformation (not information). So to be aware of being is to be feeling/experiencing being (not knowing of it) and, in that experience, being transformed by what being is.

CHAPTER THIRTY-FOUR

When you find yourself
Cultivating the growth
Of awareness
In order to discover
The more-ness of the quality
Of the messages conveyed
By the laws of life,
You will come upon
A more significant
Way of experiencing
The multiple dimensions
Of that life
Through which
You experience
The life you participate in.

Commentary on Chapter Thirty-Four

This chapter is distinguishing your life from the life in which you participate. One is like the ocean; the other is like you within that ocean (as in the Buddhistic metaphor).

Multiple dimensions are in both of those lives. Experience of those multiple dimensions is arrived upon when one has known the laws of life and the messages derived from them. This results from acquaintance with the "more-ness" (quality versus quantity) of those messages. All this concatenation of events ensues by cultivating the growth which awareness lends to us.

CHAPTER THIRTY-FIVE

One tunnel exists
Which takes you to one brink,
The brink where
Eternity is.

That tunnel exists
Inside of you.

In the instant before
You close your eyes
You are at the mouth of that tunnel.

As soon as you close your eyes
Your consciousness
Opens into the tunnel
Which goes all the way down
To quietness and
To stillness and
To oneness.
When you are in the awareness
Of all three of these three
You are in the tunnel
Leading to where all that is
Is
In the silent motionlessness
Of eternal
Oneness.

Commentary on Chapter Thirty-Five

Here, the imagination is invoked to picture the facsimile of a science-fiction wormhole — one of those passageways that science fiction writers call on to imagine travel across space in a way that enables the traveler to go through galactic distances faster than the speed of light and thus arrive at destinations in a matter of a twinkling of an eye.

The facsimile in this chapter takes one to the very brink of eternity as if it were both light years away and immediately accessible. Paradoxical!

The second stanza reveals that this tunnel is within the self and the third stanza reveals that one is at the mouth of this would-be wormhole as soon as one's eyes are closed.

One's consciousness is then "seen" going through ordinary awareness to quietness and then stillness to oneness (the experience of oneness). When oneness is arrived upon, one is in spiritual awareness. This is another way of expressing that ordinary awareness morphed into a spiritual awareness is the ability to experience realities of the spirit.

"Oneness" is a reality of the spirit world. It manifests "All that is." It is a manifestation of "All that is." To experience oneness does not mean to understand oneness; it is to be aware of its presence.

This awareness leads to apprehension of the mystery described as "silent motionless eternal oneness," but not to the comprehension of it.

"Motionless" is intended to convey — not the going in and out of existence — but that existence "just is."

The phenomenon referred to here as "spiritual awareness" is what spiritual writers ascribe to the experience of contemplation that takes one's consciousness to a state separate from the space/time continuum; i.e., it is an alternate state of consciousness. That same phenomenon is observed by hypnotherapists when a person arrives upon self-hypnosis — a trance state that occurs when brainwaves are in what electroencephalograms denominate as the theta state. Common garden observers call the exact self-same phenomenon a daydream. There is objective scientific evidence for the existence of this alternate state of consciousness, and there are various other ways of arriving upon it besides going to silence and stillness. However, silence and stillness are "real" wormholes.

CHAPTER THIRTY-SIX

In order to contemplate life
One does well to contemplate only
The moment
In which all moments exist
And that moment is
This one
Right here and now
For all that is
Exists right now
And right now
What is is all that is
Thus:
All moments are in the here and now
Of the moment in existence
Which you can choose to contemplate
In order to be in the contemplation
Of life:
Your own
And the one in which your own
Participates,
In that order.

Commentary on Chapter Thirty-Six

Chapters Two, Six and Ten of this anthology have introduced the theme of the eternity of the moment. The added dimension, in this narrative, of a meditative experience illustrates that the moment — which we are free to focus on in a phenomenological manner — can take a person to an experience of their own life and an awareness of the larger life in which we participate.

It is not about thinking of life; it is about experiencing the life of the moment.

CHAPTER THIRTY-SEVEN

And when you are finding yourself
Focusing your time and your energy
In order to consciously experience
That ever so simple motion
Of your chest going up and
Your chest going down
As rhythmic air goes in
And some air comes out
And you literally feel the up
As well as the literal down
In the sensation of in
And its counterpart out
In the self-same experience
You can awaken to the awareness
Of the conversion of oxygen
From ordinary air
To the breath of conscious life:
Your consciousness deriving life
From the conversion of oxygen
To breath that is alive.
A transformation process ensues
From this motion traced and this
Rhythm seized
And this conversion immersion
And the transformation's source
Is the experiencing of Being itself
In the simple state of becoming.

Commentary on Chapter Thirty-Seven

This narrative extols the simple natural act of "breathing with awareness," and how doing this opens up a natural experience to a level above the natural; i.e., the inhalation of oxygen is transformed into exhalation of living breath! The alchemist would say: you are turning something material into something spiritual.

The "motion traced" captures the motion of the chest, the "rhythm seized" is the dual experience of "in" and "out" and the "conversion immersion" is simply experiencing existence immersed in oxygen that is going to breath — breath that is living in the state of becoming.

CHAPTER THIRTY-EIGHT

From one wavelength of energy
Flows force,
From force issues power
And from power
Emerges strength,
Strength becoming
Becoming like unto kundalini
Manifesting also Tao
Which translates into grace
Whence there is light
And that erupts into Being
And from Being comes the life
Which your awakened self
Experiences in the awareness
Of the wave length of energy
Which coupled
From your mother's tribe
With the wave length of energy
From the tribe
Which transmitted life
To your father.

Commentary on Chapter Thirty-Eight

Everything in the material universe, quantum physics tells us, can be reduced to atoms, quarks and "wavelengths." That wavelength, science tells us, can then become a particle of matter (i.e., in the space/time continuum) or remain pure vibrating energy (i.e., in another plane of existence which is non-measurable with any human-made instrument).

The narrative to this meditative experience simply begins with that first "wavelength" and from there, by sheer (subjective) word association, takes the reader to "force," to "power," to "strength," to "becoming like unto kundalini" (which is a powerful human energy), to "manifesting Tao" (all by word association, still), to "grace," to "light," to "existence" (being), to "life" and then to "awakened self." The narrative proceeds from wavelength to awakened self by the power of subjective word association — no scientific connection implied.

The awakened self is then experienced as coming into existence from the wavelengths of energy that have come from the mother's genes coupled with genes from the father's tribe. Ultimately, what is subtly intimated (suggested) here is that the awakened self realizes that he/she had wavelengths for parents.

CHAPTER THIRTY-NINE

What is is Being
All that is is right now

Power exudes from Being
Power to attract and power to repel.

Only Being can attract Being
Only Being can repel Being.

All that is
Is exuding attraction and repulsion
Right now.

This momentous dialectic
Of unimaginable pulling
With sheer ontological force
And pushing with opposing, equally
Unfathomable strength
Gives birth to perpetual
Becoming within Being
Rendering the omnipresent eternal
Permanence
With the (paradoxical)
Essence of impermanence:

Impermanence within permanence
In the right now of eternity
And
In the eternity of right now.

Commentary on Chapter Thirty-Nine

The first line simply states that another way to say "being" is to say "what is." The second line simply states that all that exists does, in fact, exist right now — this very instant. It is ordinary awareness telling us this. The second stanza makes an assertion about what is in existence; that is, that power is exuded from what is in existence and that that power either attracts or repels; i.e., it pulls or pushes.

The third stanza further asserts that only an existent reality has this dual power. The fourth stanza goes on to observe that the dual power of pulling and pushing is going on this very (and in every) instant because that is what being does; it attracts unto itself or it repels from itself.

The dual power is then put in the category of a momentous dialectic, a dialectic of ontological force. It is that ontological force which is at the heart of "becoming." All of the above is one way to be talking of the observable phenomenon that permanence and impermanence are paradoxically co-existent in all "that is" and all that is becoming.

The final observation is that this truth about "being" is an eternal truth.

CHAPTER FORTY

And when you are moved
To move
To what purpose of life is all about
Go to the inside
Of your own inner space
To experience explicitly: Being
In order to experience the meaning of Being
In your own being
Knowing that you can only find
Meaning about being
By going to Being itself
And while you are in the vastness
Of Being
You will be experiencing the vastness of life
And, therein, you will feel
— as if by intuition —
A purpose to life:
Your life.

Commentary on Chapter Forty

The assumption is made that everyone eventually, for the first time, is prompted to ask what every philosophical system and established religion first tries to establish, namely: What is the purpose of life?

The narrative of this chapter directs the searcher (reader) with such a question to enter one's own inner space via reflection (contemplation and/or meditation) in order to become aware of one's own being — one's own existence.

While in that awareness, the directive continues, extend the aware-state; only by being in awareness of one's existence can one be led to experience what being really is. Anything short of this does not lead to the real meaning of existence. One thing strongly implied by this is that "awareness of being" means experiencing the reality of existence and not merely forming some abstract idea or concept about it.

The searcher is further directed to appreciate that when one is "in being" one is "in vastness" like no other vastness. For, in the experience of being, one is experiencing all which that pertains to and all that happens to pertain to all existence; namely, one is experiencing the vastness of life.

Somewhere in that vastness, a purpose to life will just be intuited. It is to be noted that when one is in state of heightened awareness one is in an altered state of consciousness. That altered state constitutes a trance. To be in a trance state is to be experiencing a "knowing" that is deeper/higher than the "knowing" of ordinary consciousness.

This "knowing" comes via intuitiveness. Via intuitiveness one can arrive upon a purpose in life and it happens as a consequence of: 1. intuiting existence 2. the vastness of existence 3. the equating of existence to life 4. appreciation that the vastness of life contains purpose.

In essence, the lesson this chapter teaches is that, in the experience of the vastness of "being" (its incomprehensibility), one is actually in the apprehension of how vast life is (but not the comprehension of it) and that in that experience one can intuit that purpose in life is primarily "to be" and not necessarily "to do."

CHAPTER FORTY-ONE

For years I kept looking for
The purpose and meaning
Of life and for
Things that happen
And for the secret
Of what it's all about
And I searched
Between the covers of
The Bible and
Underneath that rock
And in the bottle and
Raked over a number
Of isms
Only to find one great source
Of discovery
Just in the contemplation
That reality, just is.

And when I stay with
That contemplation
I find me going
Deeper and deeper
Into my own inner space
And there I find myself
Experiencing a profound
But I mean, a profound
Quietness.

And such a stillness!

And all this melds into
A oneness
And in the oneness
I go to a state of Being
Wherein I need no explanation
To any of what is
Nor any explanation
About purpose or meaning
For in that state
Of Being,
I just am.

And when I just am
My awareness awakens
With ease to the simple reality
That the big bang
Is still going on,
That Being is becoming right now,
That eternity is already here
And I have the distinct awareness
That I am part and parcel of:
     1. big bang
     2. becoming Being and
     3. of eternity already

By all means,
You
Peruse: Between the lines
     Between the pages
     Between the covers
Of scriptures and books and scrolls
Which sit in the sections
For sacred writings
In secret and public libraries
And do look under stones
— turned and unturned —
And look in the bottle and
Dare, if you will,
To visit the visions
Which hallucinogens
Can take you to and

Delve, by all means,
for the metaphors
In classic novels and
Search the heart
Of world-class poetry and
Hear the lyrics of moving music
Which promise omens,
Go to these: Fonts and
              Springs and
              Wells and
              Treasure troves
In your pursuit for light,
Just don't forget
That one revelatory source
Which is
The sacred space inside of you

The space you take
Wherever you take
Your mind, body and spirit,
The space made sacred
By the opening up
Of your awareness
To sheer quietness
And to
Ontological stillness
The space made sacred
By the melding
Of
The quietness within
With
The stillness of "what is."

The place to which
I am reminding you to go
Becomes a place of: Revelation
              Enlightenment
              Inner vision
Because
In there inside of you
In the presence of your own Being

You won't forget
To experience your experience
You can't forget
To experience your experience
You simply experience your experience
The experience whom you are;
And that is without an
Epistemological doubt
And encounter with
Incontrovertible Being.

Commentary on Chapter Forty-One

The visual presented in the first sentence is of a searcher looking for the secret of life. That searcher goes through the Bible's pages and to innocuous places and to alcohol highs and through the ism's of science and philosophy only to find that — all along — the answer to life's secret lies within one's self as one is contemplating that existence just is! Meaning that: existence does not explain itself as to its origin. It simply appears to our apprehension.

The narrative instructs, however, that, in staying with that theme of reality's presence (i.e., "reality just is"), one goes deeper and deeper into ordinary awareness and, in doing so, one penetrates profound quietness and stillness (presumably of being). One experiences those aspects of existence (being) melding into the experience of oneness. By this time, the searcher is beyond ordinary awareness and is experiencing reality in the realm of the spirit (i.e., beyond matter). The searcher is experiencing spiritual awareness.

At this/that point the searcher senses that some transformation has occurred. He/she senses that he/she is in awareness of a reality that is beyond the need for explanations about purpose or meaning. There, the searcher "just is" — just exists (as does the present). This is intended to mean that the searcher's awareness has awakened to a superior way of being aware. Contemplatives like Father Thomas Keating would call this a spiritual awareness.[3] That state awakens one to the contemplation of realities such as: 1. the Big Bang's ongoing-ness 2. being and becoming, as well as, 3. eternity and 4. the searcher's place in all of that.

The next visualization of this narrative is of you the reader going as a searcher yourself to peruse between the lines, the pages and the covers of all matter of writings (regarded esoteric and above the mundane) in order to look/search in stupors of hallucinogenic experiences and explore the metaphors of classic novels and poetry as well as majestic

---

[3] Cynthia Bourgeault, *Centering Prayer and Inner Awakening.* Cowley Publications, 2004: page 10.

music (whatever promises to be a font, a spring, a well or treasure-trove capable of shedding light on your search).

See yourself questioning if you must; just do not forget you are reminded: the sacred space within you is a place to search for the meaning of life. A description follows on how the sacredness of your inner space derives from the ordinary awareness of quietness and stillness and how it happens that that ordinary awareness graduates to a quietness and stillness of ontological proportions.

At that point you will be in revelation — in enlightenment — in inner vision.

In that state, the narrative concludes, by being present to your own presence you are in the equivalency of being aware of being. This is not ordinary awareness; it is knowing being by being in being; i.e., you cannot know being outside of being. (Some would say that it is experiencing the paradox of Being without the angst of Becoming).

CHAPTER FORTY-TWO

In order to visit the frequency
Where Being can be perceived
As its vibrant self
One needs to vibrate to the frequency
Enjoyed by
Unmitigated stillness and
Clear cool quietness
And
To vibrate to these frequencies
Requires us to be open
To what Being can do.

It is the awareness of Being
Which awakens one
To the presence of
Ontological quietness
And Ontological stillness.
The one awakening of
These two experiences of Being
Turns on the light of
Illumination
Known as enlightenment by some.

One does not bring on illumination.
It happens.
It occurs when one learns to be open
To what Being can do.
This simply means that:
The "being open" in this instance

Means
Staying present
To the quietness and
To the stillness of Being itself.

The illumination
Will just be
And
When it is, one is aware that
One is vibrating
At the frequency of Being,
Perceiving Being
As its vibrant self.

Commentary on Chapter Forty-Two

The glaring presumption immediately apparent in the first few words of this narrative is that one's "being" is vibrating. Given that quantum physics can establish that any material reality can be reduced to atoms, electrons, protons, neutrons, quarks and hedrons and, ultimately, wavelengths of vibrating energy, this assumption is not gratuitous but founded in fact. The narrative unequivocally states that it is possible to visit the frequency of that vibration and that to do so, one needs to vibrate to the frequency of the still and the quiet - another bold assumption.

Vibrating to the frequency of the still and the quiet is a poetic way of suggesting that one tunes in to being in stillness and in quietness. That is ontological stillness and ontological quietness. One is led to believe that it is possible to vibrate as stillness and quietness do, when one is open to what "being" can do. In other words, "being" itself (not one's intellect) takes us to that experience of vibrating — some heady stuff.

Ah! Then the reader/searcher is instructed: when one is in the awareness of "being" (and not just conscious of "being"), one awakens to "being's" stillness and quietness. And, it is in this awakening of these two vibrating aspects of "being" that one is "put" in illumination.

It is like a light is turned on with which one can now "see" something heretofore not visible to us.

"Seeing" in this context means "feeling" with an intuiting vision and not with the physical senses. It entails experiencing a reality of a dimension different from the physical. The paradox is that that spiritual reality is present in everything physical, just as quantum physics posits that wavelengths are the ultimate in everything material.

CHAPTER FORTY-THREE

You
Are a thought
Generated by the Eternal Consciousness,
You
Area a word spoken into existence
By the Eternal Consciousness,
You
Are an act designed
By the Eternal Consciousness,
You are a manifestation of
The Eternal Consciousness.

It has been given to you
To be as significant as is:
One leaf
Any leaf in the universe.

The parallelism between you and that one leaf
Is that you both have the power
To transmit life itself.
The leaf accomplishes transmission
— of life —
Through the emission of oxygen
Giving, thereby, cellular life
To the living.
You accomplish the transmission of life
Through the thought you generate,
Through the word you speak,
Through the act you design,

Through the manifestation of
The Eternal Consciousness
Whose awareness
Your awareness proclaims.

Commentary on Chapter Forty-Three

The main theme of this meditation is to situate the reader/listener in his/her place in the hierarchy of the created universe.

For the sake of contemplation, you the reader/listener are signaled out to be a thought, a word, an act — one generated, spoken and designed by the Eternal Consciousness. And, as such, you are designated as a manifestation of the Eternal Consciousness. You are an exalted place in the hierarchy of the created universe.

In quick succession to this, you are characterized to be as significant as is a leaf — any leaf (not a forest or a tree, but a leaf)!

Then comes, not only the reason for the parallelism to the leaf but the significance of the parallelism: both you and the leaf stand out as transmitters of life itself (presumably, as is the Eternal Consciousness).

At that point, the place in the hierarchy of creation rises even more for the leaf and for you.

Further, for the sake of contemplation, the leaf's power to transmit life is shown in its process of photosynthesis; whereby, oxygen is generated (by the leaf) and is destined to be the food for the cells of living organisms. Your power to transmit life is delineated as the ability to have the same energy emanate from you as has been emanated to you from the original source. Your transmission of life becomes an enfolded emanation of energy through thinking your thoughts and speaking your words and executing your actions; all of which liken you (by analogy) to the original Generator, Speaker and Actor from whom you flow.

And then your awareness has the power to proclaim the awareness of the original Thinker, Speaker, Actor.

That is how you transmit life itself: by emanating the energy that emanated to you from the original Source.

CHAPTER FORTY-FOUR

One contemplation
That can propel you
Into a propitious meditation
Is to consider what that one sage
Points out to us
When he calls attention
To our standing on the edge
Of a beach
And we, seeing what we report
As a vast ocean,
When, in reality,
What we perceive then
And what stretches out before us
Are two so very distinct things
That we have to nod assent
To that philosopher of old
Who wisely observed:
"the senses indeed sometimes deceive."
For what we perceive, is
A one — one ocean —
When, in fact,
What truly lies in front of us
Is a multitude
Of millions of billions
Of entities so infinitesimally small
That our visual sense
Is not microscopic enough
Nor sufficient to see
That those
trillions of quadrillions

Of entities
Which in the millions of billions
Exist
As molecules of water
And atoms — two hydrogen to every one
Oxygen —
And (the entities)
In the trillions and quadrillions
Are the further broken down
Into the subatomic particles
Which we call
Hadrons and quarks and
Then ultimately wave lengths —
Wave lengths of energy.

That is the reality in front of us
At that beach:
Reality in such minute form
That we cannot see it,
So our mind interprets
The vision before us
As: one ocean.

This contemplation
Deepens
To depths of
Ontological awe
When, by extension
Of what we intuit about Being,
We imagine
With our fantastic ability
To travel inwardly
And picture ourselves
Walking on the edge
Of our very own Milky Way
And gaze
At what our mind
Interprets as
One vastness of one galaxy,
Again calling
A "one"

When, in fact and
In that tableau,
What is existing in reality
Are millions and billions
Of what we call stars;
And the trillions and quadrillions
Before us are the satellites and moons
Of those bursting balls of fire
All of which our mind interprets
The way the entirety is perceived,
Namely, as a one something.

It's enough to make us wonder
How we can even contemplate
The sheer enormity of what, in fact,
Exists before us
When we peer
Through the computers
That peer
Through a Hubble telescope
And "see"
Millions of galaxies
In just one of the segments
Of one of the corners
Of one of the quadrants
Of the infinite-looking vastness
Which is, paradoxically,
So big
That we cannot see it.

In all humbleness,
We acknowledge that
It's one thing
To be unable
To see
The "so minuscule;"
It's quite another
To be unable
To see
The "so vast."

Indeed the senses do deceive.

Fortunate for us
That we do not have
Only the five physical senses.
The real consisting
Of one entirely perceived
Material universe
Made up of
Individual wavelengths of
Energy
Not a one of which
Can we: see nor
: smell nor
: feel nor
: taste nor
: touch
But all together
We perceive them
Constituting a one,
A one material universe
Present to
Our mental vision's
Apprehension.

Enough to make us wonder, too,
What other dimensions
There are and are there
To the real besides the material.

Fortunate enough for us indeed!
That we have more than
The five physical senses with which to apprehend
"The real."

Commentary on Chapter Forty-Four

This theme is presented as if a contemplation can lead to a (propitious) meditation. Many would argue that it is a meditation which could lead to a propitious contemplation. Here, the terms are used interchangeably and not as the main topic. The sage alluded to in line four is anyone from the physical sciences who knows how to scientifically demonstrate that all matter can be reduced to molecules (the smallest part of a substance which retains the properties of that substance) and that beyond the molecule there can be further division into atoms and beyond that into electrons and protons and neutrons and from there into hedrons and quarks — only to arrive upon wavelengths as the ultimate. Wavelengths, we are instructed by science, can be a particle of matter (the smallest we can arrive upon) or it can be a vibration; i.e., it is a reality belonging to a level of existence beyond the space/time continuum. It is called non-local by some. It is called spiritual by some. The "philosopher of old" in line 16 alludes to the school of philosophy which argues that our senses deceive us enough that we cannot, with certainty, declare that what we see, feel, taste, smell or hear exists in objective reality. Their mantra is that what we sense is delusion. Their school is the School of Skepticism.

With this as a background, see that this narrative speaks to the wisdom of the "philosopher of old" whose viewpoint is proved true by the wisdom of the sage.

This narrative does so by observing that, when we stand before the Pacific Ocean or the Atlantic we "see" what our mind interprets as a "one," when in reality what exists does so in such minute form that our physical vision is not capable of seeing the water molecules — much less the atoms and the parts of the atoms and the quarks and hedrons and (absolutely definitely) not the wavelengths. The glaring implication is: because we cannot see the "so minuscule," we tend to ignore its existence and we are inclined to believe (with firm conviction) that our idea of a "one" exists objectively.

The narrative then takes us to imagining that we can actually walk along the edge of our galaxy. Here we would do exactly what we do at the edge of an ocean; we would see one Milky Way when, in fact and in that instance, the "one" is composed of the many solar systems; i.e., one galaxy is made of suns and satellites too small for us to see. The galaxy is so vast that our vision cannot take it all in. We cannot see the layers.

It would be a travesty to not be aware of the parts of the galaxy or the elements of these parts. By extension, what is in the tableau which a Hubble-like telescope can see is called "one" quadrant of endless space. That quadrant is composed of so many galaxies that we cannot see them all. The lesson here is not about physics but about the fact that we are literally surrounded by both the "so minuscule" and the "so vast;" we cannot apprehend much less comprehend our environment. Small wonder that the physical sciences have concluded that we only know about four percent of what exists in the physical universe (of which we know something about); 96% of the universe eludes us 100%!!

The final one-two punch of this narrative: we go on to perceive "one" universe when in reality — though it may act as "one" — it, too, is composed of individual wavelengths in numbers beyond our pay grade to apprehend (much less comprehend).

All these un-maskings of illusions lead us to wonder what other dimensions may exist besides the material which we barely apprehend.

Note is taken that we have more ways to deal with the real than through the medium of the five senses and through ways and means beyond induction and deduction. Mystics and yogis have been experiencing for centuries what that beyond is.

CHAPTER FORTY-FIVE

Observe the sea
Try to see the rising sea

It rises in the form of vapor —
Water in liquid form
Converted to gas by heat.

The rising invisible vapor molecules
Coalesce
To become a visible cloud.

The presence of the cloud
Betrays
The rising which we cannot see.

Observe the cloud
Which a moment ago
Existed in the form of sea
And see how it travels overhead
Moved by the winds
To any of the four corners.

Your vision will catch
The white vapor clouds
Joining clouds of dust
Made up of tiny, tiny particles
Particles of matter
Too small to have much weight

But when cumulatively taken
And when joined to vapor
Become too heavy to stay aloft
And so
The darkened cloud
Begins to descend and descend
And, as it falls through less heat,
The vapor resumes
Its original shape
The shape of water
In the form of falling rain
And in this manner
Tons and tons of water
Fall and fall
And hit the earth
running
Running to become
Rising lakes
Or rivers on the run
Snaking their way
To the nearest sea
Whence the water molecule
Once was.

Expect, too,
That there will be scenarios
Where the descending, darkened vapor
Will cascade
Through air so cold
That the gaseous form of water
Turns to water in the solid state
Of ice
And in that scene
Water is hitting earth
In the form of hail
Or sleet
At times becoming flakes
Flakes of snow
Neither ice nor liquid
But snow
And it glides to earth

And soon with the help
Of heat sufficient
That ice or sleet or flakes of snow
Transmogrify to rivers or lakes
Only to head toward that state
Where water can ascend
Once more
In the form of
— you guessed it —
vapor to become, once more,
clouds
and in that form
the winds will continue
to move tons of water
from one sector of the globe
to another one.

What if
What if this observable
Circular process is a: sign,
                    A metaphor,
                    A paradigm
That, first,
There is an eternal intelligence
And what if
The: sign
       metaphor
       paradigm
Hints that we
The observers of the process
Are the temporal intelligences
Who derive what we are
From that from whom
We emerge.

It could then mean
That in due time,
As the course of things goes,
We, too, shall return
To the source of the force
From whom we came

Just
Like the molecule of sea water
Went to vapor molecule
To ice or snow or sleet
Or plain rain.

Who knows what
The omen portends.
But it does seem to feel
Like we are joined
To a particle of matter
Which is weighing us down
Just enough
To enable us
To descend
To where we can naturally flow
To the nearest...

Where was it we came from
When we were
First ascending
In intelligence?
In consciousness?
In awareness?

Commentary on Chapter Forty-Five

In this narrative the marvel of the transformation in nature is quickly seen by the naked eye of the beholder while the water molecule (the smallest part of a substance retaining the qualities of that substances as witnessed in Chapter 42) moves from the liquid of ocean water to the the form of vapor rising to the shape of a cloud and then to the shape of a rain drop. Alternatively, in colder temperatures, we see that molecule take on the shape/form of ice or sleet or snow only to descend to earth melted and liquid once more.

This process is observed occurring across a vast geography, depending on what winds carry which clouds (water in vapor form) to which environments. It culminates in rivers and/or lakes which seek their own level (as water always does) and back at the ocean/sea level from whence the movement of the molecule of water first ascended. What is not visible to the naked eye is the power of the beholder to recognize omens, metaphors and/or paradigms for what these realities teach.

This power offers a meaning beyond the meaning of the process — just as words can carry a meaning beyond the meaning of the words. That process can lead the beholder of wonder to wonder further whether he/she and other observers might not be like molecules emanating from a superior reality (like the smallest parts of that superior reality retain the qualities of the superior reality). Since the beholder manifests the characteristics of intelligence, consciousness and awareness that beholder cannot help but believe that those qualities come from the superior from whom the beholder emanates.

Note is taken that, just as the dust particle in vapor eventually weighs the water molecules back into the sea, the observer is in a material body that, of its own accord, wears down to a last heartbeat and final breath, liberating the spirit of the human molecule to return to whence it arose! Intelligence! Consciousness! Awareness! Note well taken.

CHAPTER FORTY-SIX

Today
I want to meditate
On the Being
Who I am
So that
I can grow
In the awareness
Of the Being
From whom I come
From whom I flow
From whom I emerge
From whom I issue forth
And
From whom I become
The Being who I am
Today.

Commentary on Chapter Forty-Six

This narrative speaks of a searcher who wants to be awakened to the verb or verbs that best reveal his/her entrance into existence. The assumption is that an awakening about one's "being" (existence) will yield a clue as to whether human "being" comes, or flows, or emerges, or issues forth or becomes from another or some or all of the above.

What the searcher experiences in the state of awakening about his/her existence will determine which verb or verbs are preferred in order to form a conceptualization — not about the self — but about the source from whom the self "is."

CHAPTER FORTY-SEVEN

When you contemplate
What Zen said
When Zen says so paradoxically:
"You! Do not forget
You are unique —
Just like everyone else"

You can rightly interpret that
To reveal:
The reason
No one Being is special
Is
Because all Beings are.

And coupling that
To what the Tao Te Ching
Unfolds
When it enables us
To feel and to articulate:
"Yes! I am ordinary and
I need not be otherwise"

In the architecture of this
You can feel the emergence of
The distinctive experience:

I am both special and ordinary
I am both ordinary and unique

Both both's happening
In the same field of energy —
The one I am
In the right now of this now

And the same is applying
To all the Beings
In this energy field
Which is my reality.

Commentary on Chapter Forty-Seven

The first stanza of this meditative theme points to the paradoxical Zen-ism that each of us is unique just like, indeed, everyone else is.

The second stanza explains the above paradox with another paradox; namely, no being stands out as special because each being is just that.

The third stanza goes to the Tao to remind us that we are ordinary and we do not need to be extraordinary to be superlative.

The fourth stanza connects the Buddhist thought with the Taoist thought and the synthesis yields:

> I am both special and ordinary
> I am both ordinary and unique

(The subtlety here is in the connection of Buddhism with Taoism).

The fifth stanza sees these two streams of reality becoming the energy field from which we are.

The narrative concludes: that which applies to the individual applies to all beings in our reality. Paradoxes embrace us all.

CHAPTER FORTY-EIGHT

You
Your intuiting self
In oneness
With your eyes closed
While your limbs
— upper and lower —
Your torso, your head, neck and face
Are releasing tension
Allow yourself to be focusing
You
Your intuiting self
Being like the center of a sphere,
That center
Being in oneness
With all the points of the circumference.
For this meditation
Consider that the sun
Is a sphere
A sphere of light
A sphere of fire
A sphere which gives life
Through the energy it transmits
and note well how it is
That although we have never
Been to the center
Of the sun
Our mind can well apprehend
That that center
Is in perpetual oneness

With all points
Of its circumference.

In the mental projection
Where you can sense yourself
To be at the center of a sphere
And in touch with all points
Of that circumference
Sense, too, how you can
Imagine
That sphere extends into the reaches
Of outer space
And simultaneously into the magic
Of the familiarity
Of inner space
And feel yourself wanting
To be at one
With Being, your Being
Wanting to be at one
With consciousness, your consciousness
Wanting to be at one
With awareness, your awareness
Wanting to experience
Awareness
Of a greater awareness
In the center of your living self
Flowing through the conscious awareness
Of you
In touch with all your Being.
Be wanting to be
At one
With all that is in eternity
Right now and right here
By extending your inner self
Outwardly and inwardly
Feeling yourself moving
Omni-directionally
That you may intuit with your
Feeling self
How it simply is
That eternity

Has all of eternity
To unfold and unfurl
As eternal.
And how it simply is
That the eternity
Of the instant of eternity
Is happening
As we speak,
Thus, you can intuit
That the instant
Of eternity's instant
Is
Today
That instant touching all points of its circumference.

Commentary on Chapter Forty-Eight

This chapter is to be read as a guided meditation. This narrative (of an experience) begins with a request that you allow yourself to close the eyes and immediately start to release tension (deliberately) from limbs, torso, head, neck and face. Next (without missing a beat) you are suggested to focus in on that part of yourself which knows by intuiting and to place that intuition on the feeling of "being" at the center of a sphere. Next, you are asked to imagine that center to be immediately in touch with all parts (points) of the circumference of the sphere you are imaging to be within.

In order to facilitate this intuition, the daily sun is brought to mind. The sun — a huge sphere of light and fire — is a sphere which we can well imagine to have a center; it is a sphere that is constantly and immediately in the here and now and in touch with all points of its circumference.

The reality of perpetual oneness is also subtly brought to mind. Thrown in for good measure is the suggestion that we start out imagining in the center of our inner space and then incorporate all outer space as the area of our imaginary sphere.

Admittedly, all this calls for much creativity by one's imagination. The suggestion of releasing tension is not imaginary. More than a guided day dream, we are asked to entertain suggestions that could be engaged as wants/intentions: oneness with our being, our consciousness and our awareness.

Then, as if these suggestions were not already of huge proportion, we are asked to imagine engagement with the being, consciousness and awareness of a Higher Being. The narrative keeps rolling like a stream of consciousness that has no bounds, taking us "to be wanting to feel" being at one with everything and doing it all inside our (imaginary) sphere as if we were like sound waves arriving upon the presence of the eternal (no less!) and unfurling "as eternal." The sequence of events is happening right now, as if "right now" is the center of a sphere which reaches and touches all points of eternity.

This instant being the center of eternity!

The flow of suggestions, from start to finish, is intended to take the searcher from the state of consciousness to an altered state of ordinary awareness and then (over and above) to the state of extraordinary awareness. Some call this state spiritual awareness for, in this state, one catches glimpses (as it were) of the presence of "being" vibrating at a frequency way above the frequency of vibration in the material universe. (Aside! An electroencephalogram machine hooked onto a person at this stage of the guided meditation would probably show brain wave activity at the alpha or theta level of vibration).

Three sentences comprise this guided meditation.

Some would argue that "catching a glimpse" means experiencing those frequencies with an energy which one acquires in the contemplative process; an energy superior to the energy we experience in ordinary awareness. Epistemologists would call this state: being in the third degree of abstraction. Mystics call it: being in the state of awareness in the spirit world; i.e., it is being in spiritual awareness.

Nota Bene: This experience is one of those which can be better had when this narrative is read to the searcher or listened to in a recorded manner.

CHAPTER FORTY-NINE

Nothing brings us to awareness
Of the present
Like the present itself,
Enlightened teachers teach,
And in the same lesson
They remind us that we need not
Bother to look for magic
To penetrate the mystery
For
The mystery "just is"
— The one embedded in the present
Revealed by the awareness
Of all this "that is."

Nothing nor no one penetrates the mystery.
But even a limited mind
Can stand in its presence
And limitations notwithstanding
In the presence of the present
We experience: Quiet majesty
: Simplicity
: Complexity
: Ever-changing design and
: Apparent stillness
All "just there."

Rather than attempting to wrap our mind around it,
We let it wrap itself around us
As a mind

Perceiving it (the present) extending in all directions
Simply being in multiple dimensions
And engulfing unknown levels.
We taking in a reality
Of which we are part and parcel.

From the Eckhart Tolles of our world
We learn to teach ourselves
To observe — simply learn to simply observe.
In this act we take in what we see,
What sees us seeing it
What we hear, what we feel and where — exactly —
Do we feel it, how things taste and
What fragrances emerge and arise and
Settle in our there-ness,
Simply observing,
Neither judging
Nor having to define nor to describe
Nor call by name, nor assigning a class,
Neither a genus nor a specific difference,
All in the act
Of allowing "what is" (right now)
To simply be, as it flows
there and then — here and now
As it becomes known to us
And in that observing observance
We go to the experience of: Majesty
                       : Simplicity
                       : Complexity
                       : Ever-changing design and
                       : Apparent stillness
                       : The present as it is
And as it wraps itself around our knowing
And our growing awareness,
The present becoming conscious of itself
Through our experience of this,
Our awareness.

Commentary on Chapter Forty-Nine

The Buddhistic observation is flatly stated that "to go" to awareness of the moment one need not travel any geography with any special equipment other than engaging the moment by observing (wide-eyed) the present.

The enlightened teacher, we are reminded, has already been tempted to assign magic to what is revealed when one dares to try to penetrate the present with simple awareness of the present — only to discover that the present just exists. This revelation is quickly put in the category of mystery because, in revealing itself to "just be," it is not explained how the revelation is revealed or by whose power. And, in announcing itself to our observation, the revelation is about all that exists.

The meditation theme goes on to suggest that, despite the limitations on our ability to penetrate the mystery of the present, even limited minds can be affected by the presence of mystery. This happens when we are present to quiet majesty and that which is experienceable as simple and complex simultaneously and simultaneously in constant flux and perfectly still! The poet would say: "it is the concrete experience of the abstract in simultaneity." This calls for a willingness to face paradox head on.

The key for handling these paradoxes (which come across as contradictions — like all paradoxes do) appears in the caveat to "not attempt wrapping the mind around" what's admittedly a mystery. Rather, we are invited to allow the focused-upon-present to enfold itself around the non-comprehending but apprehending mind.

Part of what results from this apprehension is a sense that the present goes in all directions (just as the center of a sphere can go to all points of its circumference as pondered in Chapter 46). Also apprehended (and not comprehended) is the reality that the present now exists in multiple dimensions which engulf unknown levels — not foreign to mystery — including the level of our material self (hence our participation as "part and parcel").

Another key for handling the paradoxes is found in the

model of Eckhart Tolle's teaching in *The Power of Now* to observe — to simply observe.

As Tolle teaches, the narrative here advises that we need not be in a lotus position with eyes shut to penetrate the mystery of the present. In fact, the narrative clearly advises to be totally conscious of what each of the five physical senses is taking in. We are assured that, as we take in information gleaned from our senses, we will witness a flow before us of what is and what is becoming and all in paradoxical form. Note well the powerful climax of this narrative: the present, allowed to wrap itself around our knowing self in awareness (that means us in an alternate state of consciousness), enables us to experience the present as the mystery of paradoxes on one level and, on another level, to apprehend the present becoming conscious of itself through the awareness that we — as part and parcel of the apprehended present — engage in.

CHAPTER FIFTY

With the eyes of the body closed
Allow the mental vision
To peer
Into the vastness within,
Allowing the awareness
To focus on the oneness
Of that vastness.

"What is"
Is there because "it is"
And it refers to power
And power is energy
And energy is interchangeable
With life.

Life is force.
Force is the flow within.

All things flow;
All that "is" is flow-in-force
With life and is
Alive with power.

When your self is in this vastness
Of that awareness,
That intuiting self
Is thereby immersed in being
— in your being —

In the being of your life,
In the life of your being.

The vision you behold beholding you
Is the awareness of being
In awareness of being.

Commentary on Chapter Fifty

This chapter is a guided meditation pure and simple. Its contents are better understood for the experience they can render by listening to someone's voice or hearing one's own recording of the text. Read slowly.

The idea here is to allow a process to unfold as one closes the eyes and peers into the vastness within. It helps to allow one to move the closed eyes to the right, then to the left, then upwards and then downwards to simulate a survey of the vastness within. It will also help to sense a vastness of oneness (versus a vastness of nothingness).

From the experience of oneness — in whatever form or fashion— allow the self to move to how it is that what exists does so because it does.

At the same time, acknowledge that no one answer could possibly explain why existence "is" and, so, settle for "because it is." (Acknowledge the mystery at hand).

Rather than philosophize any further, allow (next in this process) the reality of existence to take you to the reality of energy and, from that, go to embark on life and how it is that all that exists.is flowing. All that exists is flowing "in flow" and flowing in force and doing so with life and aliveness of power. The guided meditation intends to bring you into this flowing consciousness in order that you may return to (experience) the vastness of the awareness of existence and power and energy — all interchangeably with life and the flow-in-force. The meditation explores immersion in — as it were — being!

The subject of the experience is awareness in "your" life and in the life of "your" being.

Finally, you are brought to an awareness of awareness. This is called the experience of a vision.

This guided meditation (like all guided meditations) suggests how to engage one's mind during meditative process. In the behavioral sciences this is called cognitive reconditioning. How one takes the suggestions and what one does with them is beyond the control of the one guiding the process. Who is in control, then? One's conscious awareness is in control.